Backyard Build Series

Board Track Motor Bicycle

Michael T Carruthers

TMC Publishing

Contents

Contents

Forward

Having worked as an Oil and Gas Engineer in Europe and Asia I decided to take some time out in Thailand. Having just finished working in China for a year and my son living in Thailand it was inevitable I would take time out in this wonderful country. Settling in Jomtien by the sea seemed to be a great idea, after a few months of the balmy heat and having done most of the things I had set out to do I was starting to go a little crazy. Having had many old British and Far Eastern Motorcycles in my youth I had always loved looking at Vintage Era Motor Bicycles. Having seen big tyre mountain bikes for the first time here in Thailand I was continually thinking how good they looked and would be even better if powered by a gas engine. My son's wife runs a bike hire shop in Jomtien so one day I tagged along to one of their suppliers in North Pattaya. I surveyed a few examples of large tyre bikes I decided that the new snow/beach tyres were just too big, I found one bike a Coyote Spin Shake, the wheel and tyre size was perfect for a vintage theme motor bicycle. I negotiated a sum of 8,000- baht approximately $220- USD. Now the hunt was on for an engine, I was not keen to strap on one of the many 2-stroke bicycle gas engines available on the internet. I walked around a few hardware stores here and found an agricultural engine and pump set which looked perfect, I was able to locate the same engine as a separate unit, a clone of the Honda GX160 5.5 h.p. 4-Stroke gas engine for the sum of 3,000 baht approximately $105- USD.

Acknowledgments

I would like to give a special thank you to all of my family and friends who helped along the way on this backyard build. My son Benjamin and his wife Noi proprietors of 'Venture Bike Hire' Jomtien, Thailand.

Thank you

Mike.

Chapter 1

The Engine

Model T55A   Motor Bicycle Technical Data

ENGINE

Type	O.H.V. Single
H.P. @ R.P.M.	5-1/2 @ 3600
Bore	68mm
Stroke	45mm
Capacity	163 c.c.
Valve Clearance Inlet	0.15 ± 0.02 mm
Exhaust	0.20 ± 0.02 mm

IGNITION

Contactless Magneto Coil

Spark Plug	*NGK* BPR6ES
Spark Plug Gap	0.7-0.8 mm

CARBURETTER

Type	PD88E
Bore	7/8in.

TRANSMISSION

Primary Drive Type	Belt Drive

Model T55A Motor Bicycle Technical Data

(Continued)

CLUTCH

Type ... ... Friction Belt

CAPACITIES

Fuel Tank ... ... 1 Gallon

Oil in Sump ... ... 0.6 Litre (20 fl.oz.)

TYRE SIZES

Front ... ... 26in. x 3in.

Rear ... ... 26in. x 3in.

SUSPENSION

Front ... ... Leaf Spring

Rear ... ... Hard Tail

BRAKES

Front ... ... Disc Rotor

Rear ... ... None

Model T55A   Right Hand Side Profile (Drive Side)

Model T55A   Left Hand Side Profile (Starting & Cooling)

GX160 Clone Engine

Having looked at a selection of Chainsaw, Bush whacker and Chinese engines, the decision was made to use a Honda GX160 clone, the purchased engine was made in japan under licence, they are also made in China. Bought from a hardware store the cost was a little over $100- USD in Thailand.

With the engine visually checked over externally, the oil level was checked by removing the filler cap/ dipstick, to my surprise there was very little oil in the sump, topping up was easy there are two filler caps either one can be used, fill with 0.6 litres (20 fl.oz.) of SAE 10W-30 oil, if topping up is required fill to the last thread of the filler hole, it is very important for the engine to be level so as not to over fill the sump.

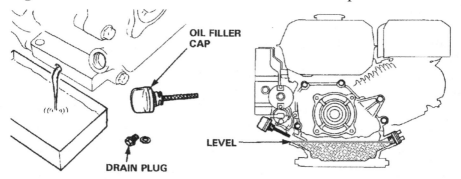

Checking the oil level.

Test Running the Engine

With the engine clamped to the workshop bench the petrol tank was filled with a small amount of petrol (gasoline). The magneto switch mounted on the cooling cowl must be switched on also the petrol tap open and the choke closed. Amazingly the engine started second pull of the pull cord. The choke was opened immediately as the ambient temperature is quite high here at home.

It was apparent upon running the engine that it was not going to be perfect in its current setup, the carburation is controlled by a governor to maintain constant speeds under load as required for its intended agricultural duties.

Removal of all the linkages springs etc. which control the carburettor butter-fly air valve were replaced with a throttle cable.

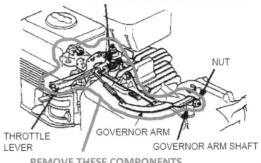

THROTTLE LEVER LIMITING SCREW

NUT

THROTTLE LEVER

GOVERNOR ARM

GOVERNOR ARM SHAFT

REMOVE THESE COMPONENTS

PD88E Carburettor

The motor still seemed to be unsuitable, a decision was made to replace the carburettor with a Honda CG110 (PD88E) slide carburettor.

The engine started first pull and idled steady at a low RPM, the throttle response was snappy, swapping out the carburettor was a good decision and brought us in to familiar territory for tuning and setting up.

Now happy that the engine works well, all of the external components were removed. To be discarded the petrol tank, muffler, exhaust manifold and heat shield were committed to the scrap box.

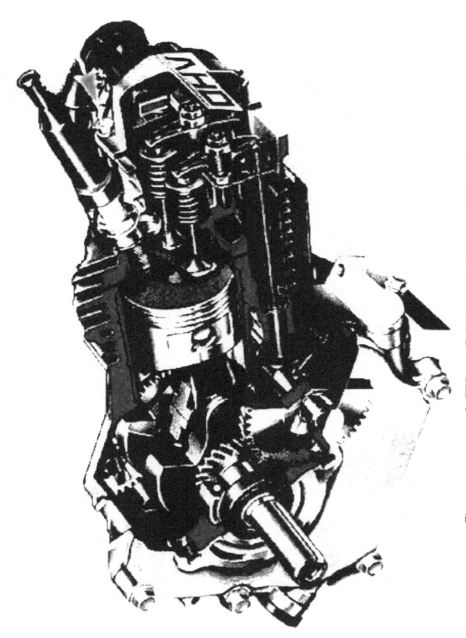

Cutaway of The GX 160 Clone Engine

Cylinder Head Components

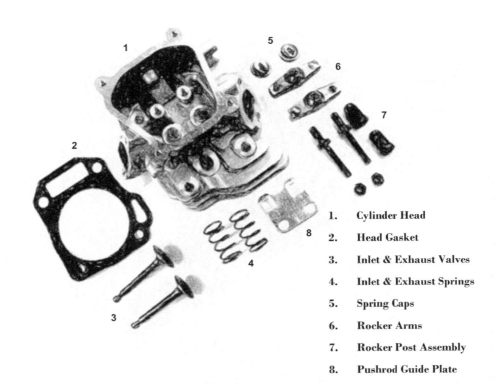

1. Cylinder Head
2. Head Gasket
3. Inlet & Exhaust Valves
4. Inlet & Exhaust Springs
5. Spring Caps
6. Rocker Arms
7. Rocker Post Assembly
8. Pushrod Guide Plate

Assembled Cylinder Head

Tappet Adjustment

With the engine cold, remove the rocker cover taking care not to damage the rocker cover gasket. Rotate the engine by hand with

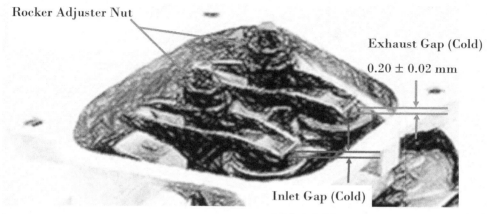

Rocker Adjuster Nut

Exhaust Gap (Cold)

0.20 ± 0.02 mm

Inlet Gap (Cold)

0.15 ± 0.02 mm

the ignition switched off and the sparkplug removed, when the inlet valve is fully open adjust the exhaust rocker adjuster nut using spanner and feeler gauge to give a gap of 0.2mm. When the exhaust valve is fully open adjust the inlet rocker to give a gap of 0.15mm.

With the rocker cover removed one engine breather modification could be made, I soldered a 1/2 brass elbow to the cover over the breather hole, tin one end of elbow with solder and tin the pe-

rimeter of the breather hole with solder. Mount the elbow so it points 45° up when installed, a small K&N mesh filter for a crankcase breather will plug nicely into the open end of the elbow.

CG 110 (PD88E)

Carburettor

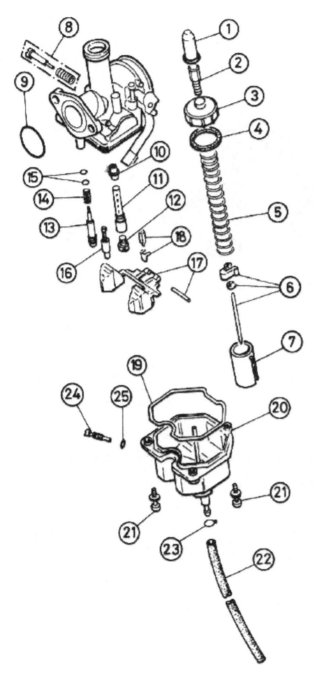

1 Rubber cap

2 Cable adjuster

3 Mixing chamber top

Gasket

5 Return spring

6 Jet needle assembly

7 Throttle valve

8 Throttle stop screw

9 O-ring

10 Needle jet

11 Needle jet holder

12 Main jet

13 Pilot screw

14 Spring

15 O-ring

16 Pilot jet

1 7 Float and pivot pin

18 Float needle valve

19 Gasket

20 Float bowl

21 Screw and washer - 3 off

22 Drain pipe

23 Clip

24 Drain screw

25 O-ring

CG 110 (PD88E) Carburettor Settings

Some of the carburettor settings, such as the sizes of the needle jet, main jet, and needle position etc. are predetermined by the manufacturer. Under normal circumstances, it is unlikely that these settings will require modification, even though there is provision made.

Pilot Screw

The throttle slide cutaway controls engine speed from 1/8 to 3/4 throttle. The size of the main jet is responsible for en-

As an approximate guide the pilot jet setting controls engine speed up to 1/8 throttle.

Idle Speed Screw

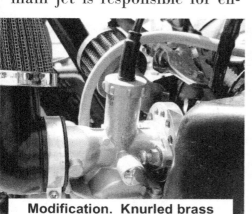

Modification. Knurled brass knob used for Idle Speed adjustment no need for screwdriver

gine speed at the final 3/4 to full throttle. It should be added however that these are only guide lines. There is a certain amount of overlap that occurs between the carburettor components involved.

Air Filter Cleaning

I have found the air here in Asia to be very dusty so filter cleaning is a regular task. Liberally spray Air Filter Cleaner onto both sides of filter and allow to soak for 10 minutes

to loosen the dirt. Do not allow cleaner to dry on air filter.

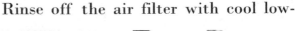

Rinse off the air filter with cool low-pressure water applied to the clean side out in order to flush the dirt out of the filter. Continue to rinse the filter until all traces of cleaner are gone. It may be necessary to repeat the process a few times.

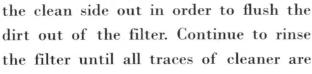

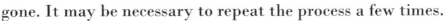

When using the air filter oil aerosol air filter oil, spray the oil evenly along the crown of each pleat holding nozzle about 3" away. Allow oil to wick for approximately 20 minutes. Touch up any light areas on either side of the filter until there is a uniform application of oil.

Spark Plug Service

Recommended spark plug: BPRGES (NGK)

WARNING!   Never use a spark plug of incorrect heat range.

To ensure proper engine operation, the spark plug must be properly gapped and free of deposits.

1.   Remove the spark plug cap and use a spark plug wrench to remove the Plug.

2. Visually inspect the spark plug. Discard it if the insulator is cracked or chipped. Clean the spark plug with a wire brush if it is to be reused.

3. Measure the plug gap with a feeler gauge.

The gap should be 0.7-0.8mm (0.028-0.031 in). Correct as necessary by bending the side electrode.

Resist tapping the plug down on a hard surface to close up the gap as this will most likely damage the porcelain insulator around the centre electrode, causing H.T. leakage and a poor spark.

Spark Plug Indications

Normal condition - A brown, tan or grey firing end indicates that the engine is in good condition and that the plug type is correct.

Ash deposits - Light brown deposits encrusted on the electrodes and insulator, leading to misfire and hesitation. Caused by excessive amounts of oil in the combustion chamber or poor quality fuel/oil.

Carbon fouling - Dry, black sooty deposits leading to misfire and weak spark. Caused by an over-rich fuel/air mixture, faulty choke operation or blocked air filter

Oil fouling - Wet oily deposits leading to misfire and weak spark. Caused by oil leakage past piston rings or valve guides

Overheating - A blistered white insulator and glazed electrodes.

Worn plug - Worn electrodes will cause poor starting in damp or cold Caused by ignition system fault, incorrect fuel, or cooling system fault weather and will also waste fuel.

Magneto Ignition

The sparks for our engine are provided by a battery-less magneto.

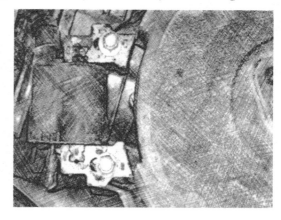

The magneto built on to engine is simply a coil wound around iron laminations, the laminates are bolted to the engine casing they have two feet which pick up a pulse from a very strong magnet mounted on the external flywheel, the induced coil produces a high voltage which is transmitted to the spark plug via a H.T. lead to the sparkplug.

WARNING!   The magneto produces very high voltages care must

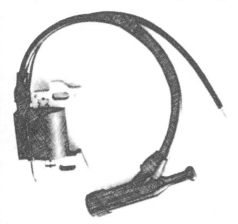

be taken even if the engine is being rotated by hand, a leak from any of the H.T. parts will give powerful shock causing injury.

A fly lead from the magneto runs back along the outside of the engine casing, this is for the kill switch, this switch short-circuits the low voltage pulse in the magneto to the engine casing.

WARNING! If you remove the switch the engine cannot be stopped.

Chapter 2
The Concept

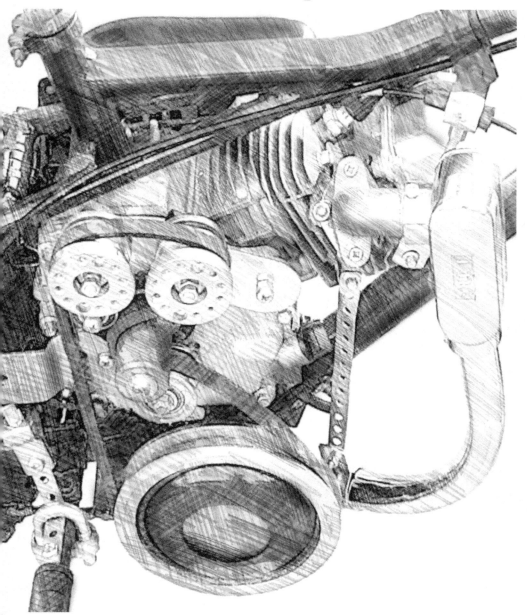

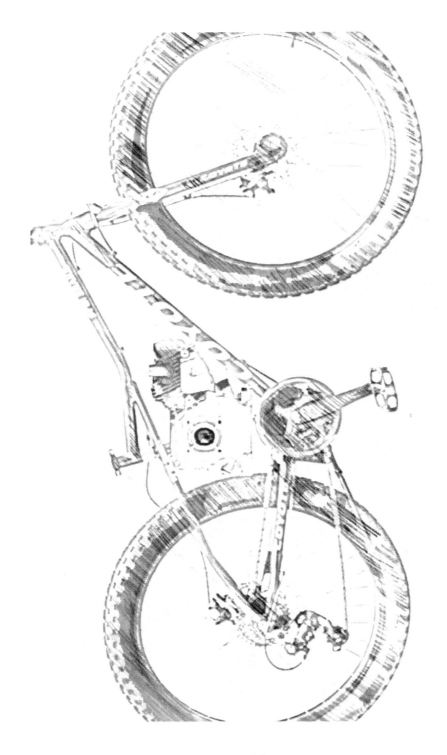

Concept Sketch

Chapter 3

The Cycle

Coyote Spin Shake Cycle

FRAME	Aluminium Alloy
FORK	High Tensile Steel
BRAKE	Disk Rotors
STEM	Aluminium Alloy
HANDLE BAR	Aluminium Alloy ZOOM
FRONT DERAILLEUR	Shimano TZ 30
REAR DERAILLEUR	Shimano ALTUS M 280
SHIFTER	Shimano EF 51
FREE WHEEL	Shimano CS HG 31
BRAKES	Aluminium Alloy PROMAX
RIMS	Aluminium Alloy Double Walled
TYRES	26in. x 3in.

The First Cut

There is no going back from this point. When we make the first cut it's a major one!. To mount the engine in the frame the seat stem tube has to be cut away. The rider's weight will be transmitted to the frame on the hard tail tubing so the loading on the seat stem is greatly reduced, even with my 16 stones the frame is holding out well. Care must be taken when cutting with the grinder as the aluminium is soft to cut and will snatch at the disc, a very firm hand is required. Safety glasses for all grinding/cutting is essential, unlike steel or iron, aluminium grindings are very difficult to remove from the eyes.

DO NOT GRIND UNLESS WEARING EYE PROTECTION!.

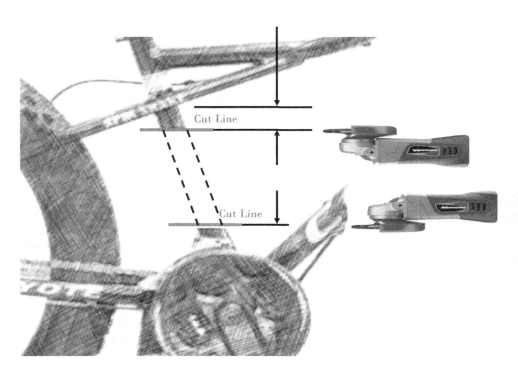

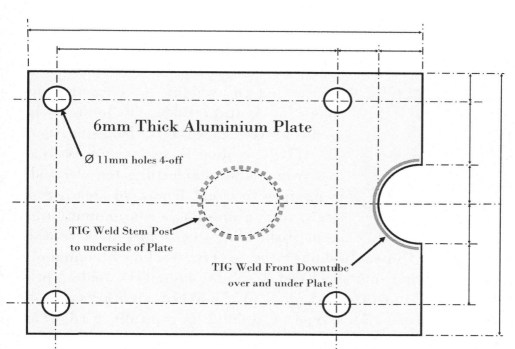

Example Aluminium Engine Mount Plate

6mm Thick Aluminium Plate

Ø 11mm holes 4-off

TIG Weld Stem Post
to underside of Plate

TIG Weld Front Downtube
over and under Plate

The engine mount plate should be made from aluminium entrust welding of the plate to someone who has access to welding equip-

ment and the correct welding rods. Do not drill the bolt holes until the welding is complete. The centreline and the cycle centreline should be the same. Aluminium checker plate is easy to find and can be use smooth side up. Clean and prepare surfaces to be welded removing paint with emery cloth the welds are fillet weld.

Welding Aluminium

I entrusted the welding to Lam the mechanic at Venture Bikes, in Jomtien, he used a process called TIG. Tungsten Inert Gas (**TIG**]) welding is an arc process that uses a non-consumable tungsten electrode to produce the weld. The weld area is protected from atmospheric contamination by an inert shielding gas. A filler metal (rod) is normally used in the welding process. TIG welding is commonly used for welding thin sheet metals, aluminium. TIG welding provides greater control over the look of the weld than other types of welding processes. This type of welding is typically used when welds will be highly visible.

Welding Steel

Welding steel is more straight forward and an easier process. I purchased a 140 Amp arc welder from the local DIY store. For 3,700- Baht around $100- USD it is an incredibly small machine compare to the Clarke Arc welder I bought 30 years ago both welding machines are rated at 140 Amps but new one is one quarter the size and totally silent. I suspect that the new one uses a toroidal transformer and electronics. WARNING! Always use the face mask and cloves do not look directly at the arc without the face mask or damage to the eyes will result in permanent scaring of the retina, headache from a flash is unpleasant.

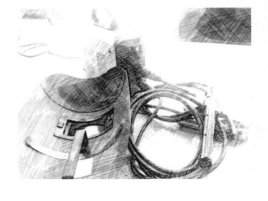

Chapter 4

Primary Drive Components

V-Belt Pulley
2-off

Gate Roller
1-off

Sealed Bearing
1-off

Cast Iron 3 groove
Compressor Pulley
1-off

Pop Rivet
6-off

Setting Up The Rear Wheel

Setting up the rear wheel requires the endless chain to be split for removal, if the chain is to be reused the task should be done using the correct tool. The same tool is used re-joining the chain our chain will need several links to be discarded. Keep all of the discarded chain parts in a packet, re-joining is quite a fiddle and often the roller pin will fall out on to the floor and be lost. I find an extra pair of hands invaluable for re-joining the chain.

Disconnect the derailleur cable, unbolt the rear derailleur from its hanger. The hanger is required for the rear wheel quick release axle so leave it in place.

Remove the rear brake cable and unbolt the brake calliper, bag all of the components for future use. Strip out all the way to the handlebars removing cables and gear selector and break lever.

Remove the rear wheel from the frame by loosening the quick release. With the wheel off the cycle undo the five allen screws holding the disc rotor onto the hub. The bolts are held fast by Loctite so the initial loosening of the screw will require the allen key to be

held firmly into the hex hole as the key will try to jump out. If the key jumps out of the hole the screw will ruined. If this happens and screw can not be taken out do not be tempted to drill it out. Use a centre punch on the side of the screw head to coax its rotation

use a medium size engineering hammer. Once the screw has moved around by a quarter turn it can be easily removed using mole-grips.

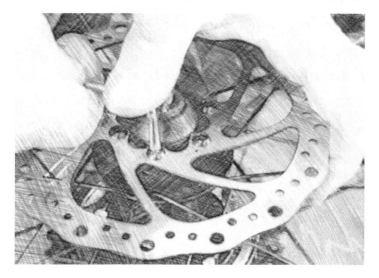

Removing The Crank Arm Assy.

Removing the crank arm assembly and pedals I would recommend you use the correct tools. The crank will be taken on and off the cycle a few times during the build. If forced to release its grip on crank pin using screwdrivers and wedges or an automotive flywheel puller damage will result to the crank assembly and bearings.

Remove bolts on both sides of the cycle using a crank spanner, it is  a thin walled chrome Vanadium steal spanner available from any good cycle shop. The bolt is threaded into the crank pin. The threads on the left side of the cycle are left-hand thread, the threads on right side of

the cycle are right-hand thread. The simple rule to remember for the crank and pedals is, to loosen any thread the spanner is  pulled up, over and rearwards, if you can imagine that both pedals are connected to spanners, pedalling will tighten and back-pedalling will loosen. To remove the 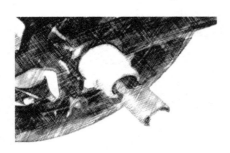 crank or pedal arm use a cycle crank puller, threads are normal right-hand threads for both sides. Hold the pedal and tighten the centre allen bolt on the puller the crank will loosen its grip on the pin with ease.

Modifying The Crank

To take the drive from the engine the crank will need a pulley, I did not want to use an aluminium pulley as the crank supplied with the cycle is made of steel. I decided to cut an iron compressor pulley to make a pulley ring, the crank was then brazed onto the pulley ring. It is very important to centre the ring before brazing, this was achieved by using six temporary rivets to hold the crank in place. The crank was mounted back onto the crank pin and spun for checking. Minor adjustments were made by tapping the pulley ring with a soft hammer. The crank was carefully removed from the crank pin for brazing. With a few spot brazes the crank was double checked. With everything looking true and aligned the crank / pulley assembly was laid on the work bench and fully brazed. Try not to braze all in one continuous run break the runs up into six smaller runs flip across and braze adjacent sections in rotation.

Compressor Pulley grinder cut along red line

Flatten out grinder marks to an even finish and thickness

Clean the cog and remove any paint on the outer cog ready for brazing

Braze along the red line flipping from side to side making short runs of braze

Modifying The Cassette

To take the drive from the crank to the rear wheel with as much reduction as can be obtained. Version 1. we are using a 53 tooth
crank cog crudely bolted to the original cassette and seems to work
well. Version 2. I have ordered a 45 tooth high reduction cassette
cog, a spacer will be made to hold this in place instead of the pre-
sent cassette assembly.

Test fit the bolts after removing small amounts of material if required, a fit without any slack is required, the bolts should be
tightened in adjacent rotation a little at a time until all tight. The
loading will be in rotational sheer mostly.

Version 2. Rear Cog

One the bench we are getting 80 km/h on the current gearing so to cruise at 50 km/h with 45 tooth cog seams to be a more relaxed pace at around 2700 RPM and a top speed of 65 km/h (40 mph)

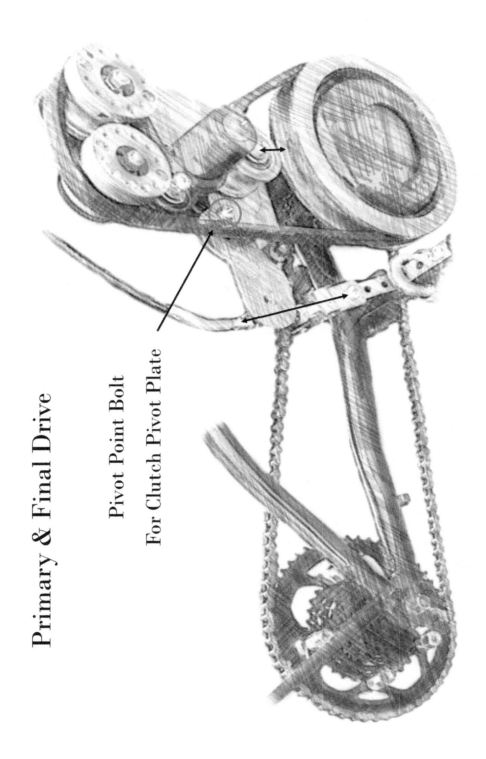

Primary & Final Drive

Pivot Point Bolt

For Clutch Pivot Plate

Primary Drive

To get drive from the engine the simplest idea was to use a belt. The engine rotates in a counter clockwise direction when viewed from the drive side, for want of a better word the engine rotates backwards compared to a normal motorcycle engine. A standard compressor "V" belt is used , drive is passed to the belt by means of a 50mm diameter shaft I had machined to a close tolerance with the crankshaft a woodruff key locks the shafts together. The belt is guided around the drive side by means of jockey wheels, these wheels were free wheeling on sealed bearings, the wheels were arranged by utilising the bolt holes on the crankcase. Four main holes on the crankcase were originally for the engine unit to be bolted to an agricultural irrigation pump used to deliver water to the rice paddy fields.

Clutch Mechanism

The clutch mechanism basically tensions the belt around the crankshaft, different sleeves were tried out on the engine crank both rubber and nylon sleeves were rejected. The rubber sleeve snatched too much when friction raised the temperature, the opposite happened when nylon sleeve was used, slipping more when hot. The final setup was an unpolished steel sleeve. The clutch pivot plate is actuated by a regular Bowden cable and handlebar lever. When the cable is pulled the pivot plate is drawn down causing the freewheeling "V" pulley wheel to tension the pulley belt tightly around the shaft.

The rotation generated in the belt is transmitted to the bottom bracket flywheel, there is no slippage between the belt and the flywheel. The flywheel in turn rotates the bottom bracket shaft, the cog set utilises the smallest cog for the final drive chain. A stainless steel chain was used for the final drive for its greater strength. The rear cog went through several stages of development, the first setup was a bolt up cog from a centre crank assembly, my son was able to track down a large rear cog with a standard cassette fastening, much safer and more reliable. The cassette can be split apart and rebuilt with the large cog on the in board side or any of the cog positions to allow a good alignment with the centre crank cog.

Rear Cog Set (Cassette)

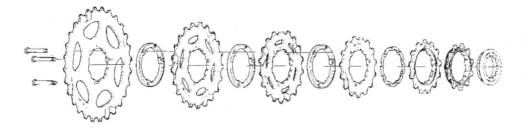

Rear Spindle (Ratchet)

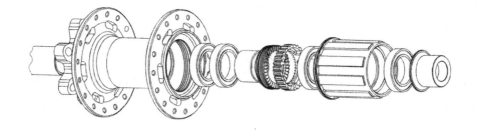

Primary Drive Components

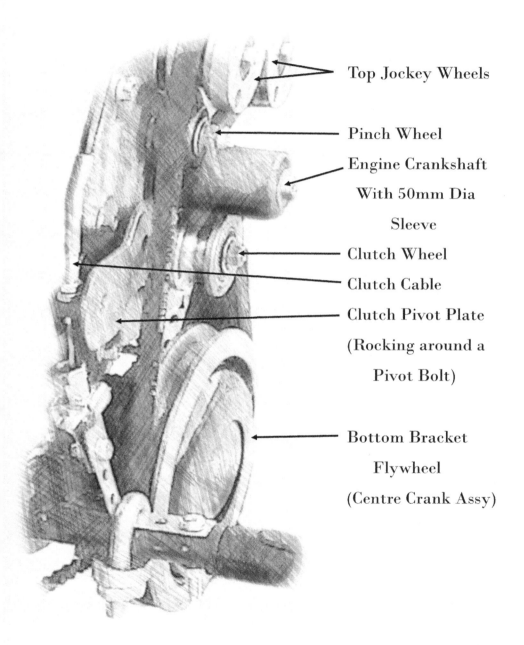

Top Jockey Wheels

Pinch Wheel

Engine Crankshaft
With 50mm Dia
Sleeve

Clutch Wheel

Clutch Cable

Clutch Pivot Plate
(Rocking around a
Pivot Bolt)

Bottom Bracket
Flywheel
(Centre Crank Assy)

Chapter 5

Engine Covers

With the engine installation complete and clutch problems ironed out, I was concerned about fingers and jeans getting caught up in

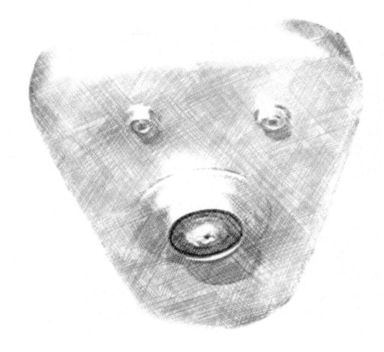

the primary drive pulley-belt. To combat this problem I fashioned a cover out of aluminium. I made a pattern first for the bolt holes and crankshaft using card. The edge of the cover was beaten over with a soft hammer to achieve a curved profile, a skirt was welded at the top perimeter of the cover, with a file and sanding sponge the weld was flush finished . The bezel for the crankshaft was made from an old aluminium lamp fitting and tack welded on the inside.

The engine is cooled by a fan, this is mounted behind the rip-cord starting mechanism. To start the engine on this bike I always intended to start it with a portable electric drill. With the starting mechanism removed and the crankshaft nut exposed it was deemed

that we had another potential stray finger problem. An aluminium plate was made to allow the drill tool to be inserted through the centre to engage with the crankshaft nut for starting. The drill tool was made from a hex bar welded to a good quality hex socket, I tried a starting crank but it whipped too much when the engine started and concern was expressed about getting a fractured wrist.

Air needs to be drawn into this cover to cool the engine so the front was prised out and beaten into shape to form a duct. The original bolt holes were utilised to fix the cover in place.

Exhaust Pipe & Silencer

The original exhaust port exits the cylinder head sideways, this is not really practical as it burnt my leg on several occasions. A Honda induction manifold was modified and bolted to the cylinder

head to point forward, the silencer was made from a high voltage cast conduit box which I had chrome plated, the inside was filled with very coarse stainless steel swarf from the machine shop. The exhaust pipe was fashioned out of a pre bend steel tube which was also chrome plated and cut off at an angle. A long stay was dropped down from the cylinder head as a steady for the exhaust pipe.

Handlebar Controls

Right Handlebar - Throttle control and front brake lever

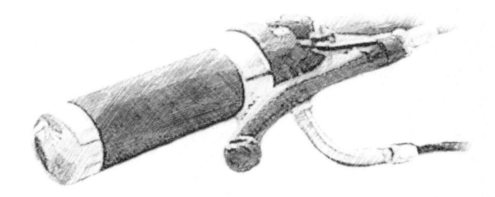

Left Handlebar - Clutch control lever

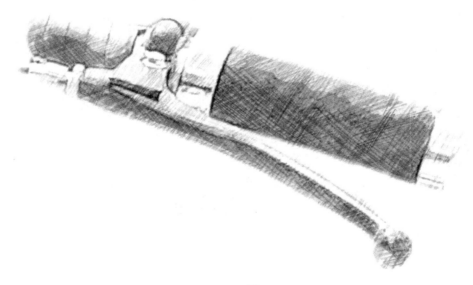

General Arrangement

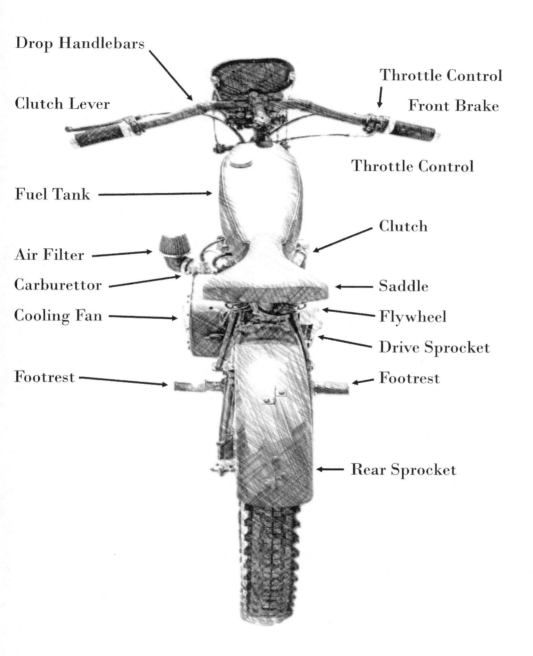

Drop Handlebars

Throttle Control

Clutch Lever

Front Brake

Throttle Control

Fuel Tank

Clutch

Air Filter

Carburettor

Saddle

Cooling Fan

Flywheel

Drive Sprocket

Footrest

Footrest

Rear Sprocket

Index

Motorcycles

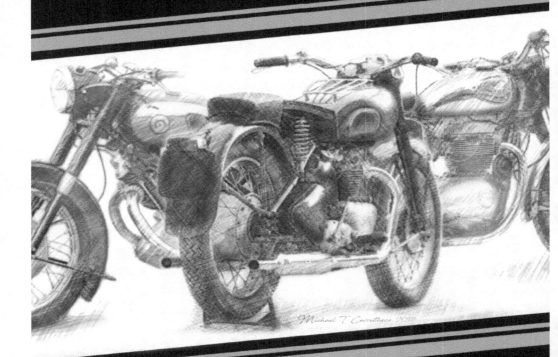

Illustrated

By Michael T Carruthers

Motorcycle
Repairs

Servicing
Tyres
Inner Tubes
Oils
Brake Pads
Forks
Chains
Bulbs

Telephone: 0939342936

Venture

รับซ่อมรถจักรยานยนต์
รับซ่อมรถมอเตอร์ไซค์

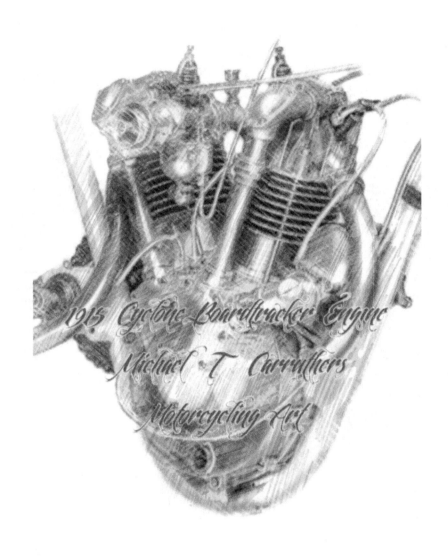

1915 Cyclone Boardtracker Engine

Michael T Carruthers

Motorcycling Art

info@rockerbox.club

www.rockerbox.club

Made in the USA
Las Vegas, NV
20 September 2022

55615323R10037